Here Come the Humpbacks!

April Pulley Sayre

Illustrated by Jamie Hogan

Charlesbridge

Flippers paddle. Flukes push.
In every ocean on Earth, humpback whales swim.

In the Caribbean Sea, male whales roll. They smack their flippers on the water. *Smack! Smack!* They blow bubbles. Their barnacled bodies bump. Their skin is scarred from past competitions.

A female humpback swims away to quiet shallows. Her blue-gray head, bumpy as a pickle, lifts and looks. It is February. She is expecting—something big, something soon. The time has come.

What's in a Name?
Humpback whales are named for the hump shape
their back makes when they dive.

Here comes a humpback!

Out, out . . . a whale calf slides from the female humpback's body. She rolls, breaking the cord that joins them. Through this cord, her body has fed him for eleven and a half months. He will have a bellybutton where their bodies were connected.

The mother lifts the calf. His pale gray head breaks the surface. But a whale cannot breathe through its mouth. The calf scoots. His blowhole meets air. *Whiss, snort!*

Whale Birth

Female humpback whales give birth
every one to four years. No scientist has
ever seen a humpback whale being born.
But scientists can imagine what happens
based on what is known about dolphin births.
(Dolphins are closely related to whales.)

Here breathes a humpback!

The calf is fourteen feet (a little over four meters) long and already weighs about a ton. He dips down, latches on, and drinks milk. Up to fifty gallons (189 liters) a day will build blubber, muscles, and energy.

The calf explores. He rubs his mother's skin. He nudges a fish's fin. He swims loop-the-loops around his mother's tail. He listens to dolphin whistles and the groans of fish. A loud song rises and rolls.

A Whale's Spout
Whales, like people, are mammals. They can't breathe underwater as fish do. A humpback surfaces, opens up its blowhole, and exhales. Air from its lungs pushes any water that is on top of its blowhole into the air. This water, plus water vapor in its breath, creates the spray we see.

Here sings a humpback!

Head down, in deeper water, a male whale sings. His song rhymes and repeats. All the male whales in the area know this year's song—yet they vary it, like jazz musicians onstage.

The calf can't sing—yet. His call is a quiet grunt. He blows bubbles that pop and hiss. He slaps his tail on the water's surface. *Splash!*

He and his mother nap. They float like logs, blowholes uncovered. A boat coasts toward the sleepy whales. Will it turn away in time?

Humpback Songs

Adult male humpback whales sing songs that can last thirty minutes. They may repeat a song for twenty-four hours or more. Male humpbacks sing mostly in warm waters during breeding season— the winter. All humpbacks make shorter, simpler calls as well.

Here comes a humpback!

An escort whale rises. He blocks the boat and slaps his tail on the water.

The captain stops her boat. Cameras click. Whale watchers stare.

The mother, calf, and escort swim away. But four shapes lurk

behind them.

Whale-Watching Rules

Conservationists and boat operators have created a set of rules to protect whales. A good boat captain never drives a boat straight toward a whale, either from in front or from behind. This way the whales don't feel chased or trapped. A good captain also avoids separating one whale from another in a group and never approaches too close to the whales. If the whales come closer on their own, that is fine.

Here come the challengers!

Four male whales approach. *Slap!* One slaps the escort whale with a flipper. *Bonk! Smack!* Two bump the escort's sides. A fourth whale pushes between the escort whale and the mother. Now they are divided.

The escort whale doubles back and pushes forward. With a lunge, he reclaims his place beside the mother-calf pair. He bumps away another male. At last the challengers peel away.

The Escort Whale

Single adult whales often escort a
mother humpback and her calf.
People used to think that the whales
were grandmothers or aunts helping
to care for the calf. But scientists
discovered that these whales are
male. The escort whale swims along
with the mother. He waits around
in case she is ready to mate.

By April, the waters are quieter. The escort whale and most other whales have migrated. But the calf and his mother still cruise the reefs. She has not eaten for six months. She is ten tons lighter than she was last May.

The mother does not have teeth for tearing, and the passage from her mouth to her stomach is small. She needs many small fish in one big bite. Those fish swim in cold waters, far, far north. It is time, at last, to migrate.

Teeth or No Teeth?

Whales are divided into two main types: toothed whales and baleen whales. Toothed whales, such as orcas, use their sharp teeth to catch fish and other prey. Humpback whales are baleen whales. Baleen is a stiff fringe that hangs down from each side of a whale's mouth. It is made of keratin, the same material that makes up human fingernails and hair. The baleen acts as a sieve to keep food in the whale's mouth as the water drains out.

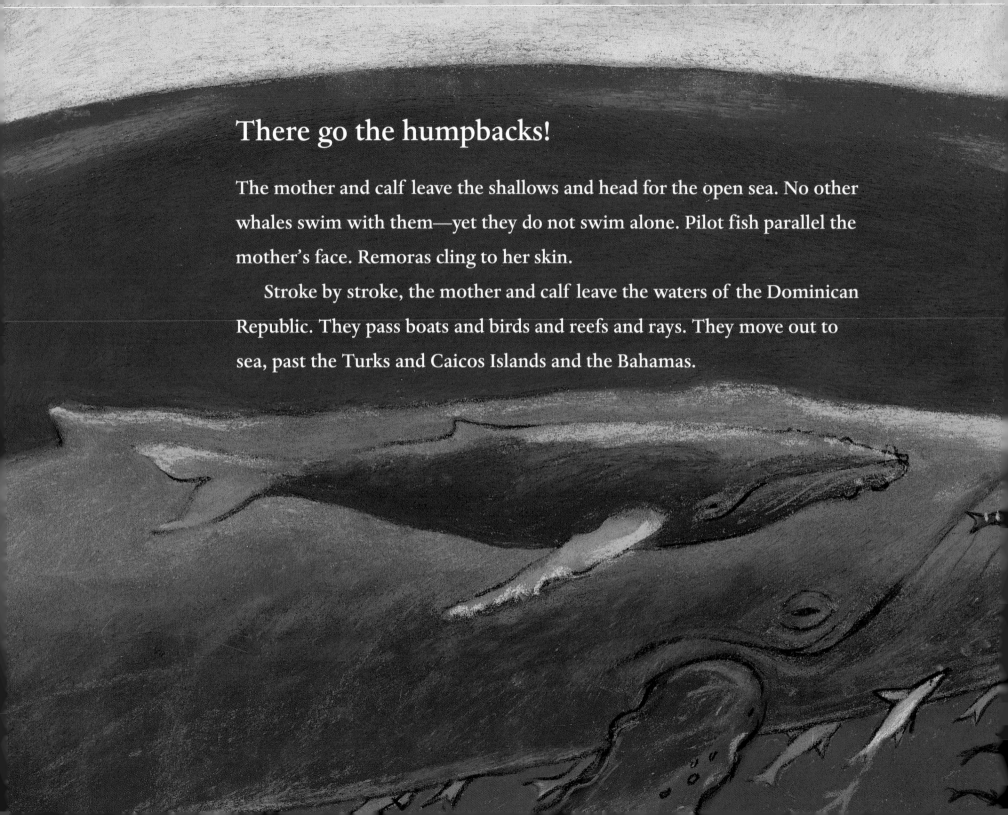

There go the humpbacks!

The mother and calf leave the shallows and head for the open sea. No other whales swim with them—yet they do not swim alone. Pilot fish parallel the mother's face. Remoras cling to her skin.

Stroke by stroke, the mother and calf leave the waters of the Dominican Republic. They pass boats and birds and reefs and rays. They move out to sea, past the Turks and Caicos Islands and the Bahamas.

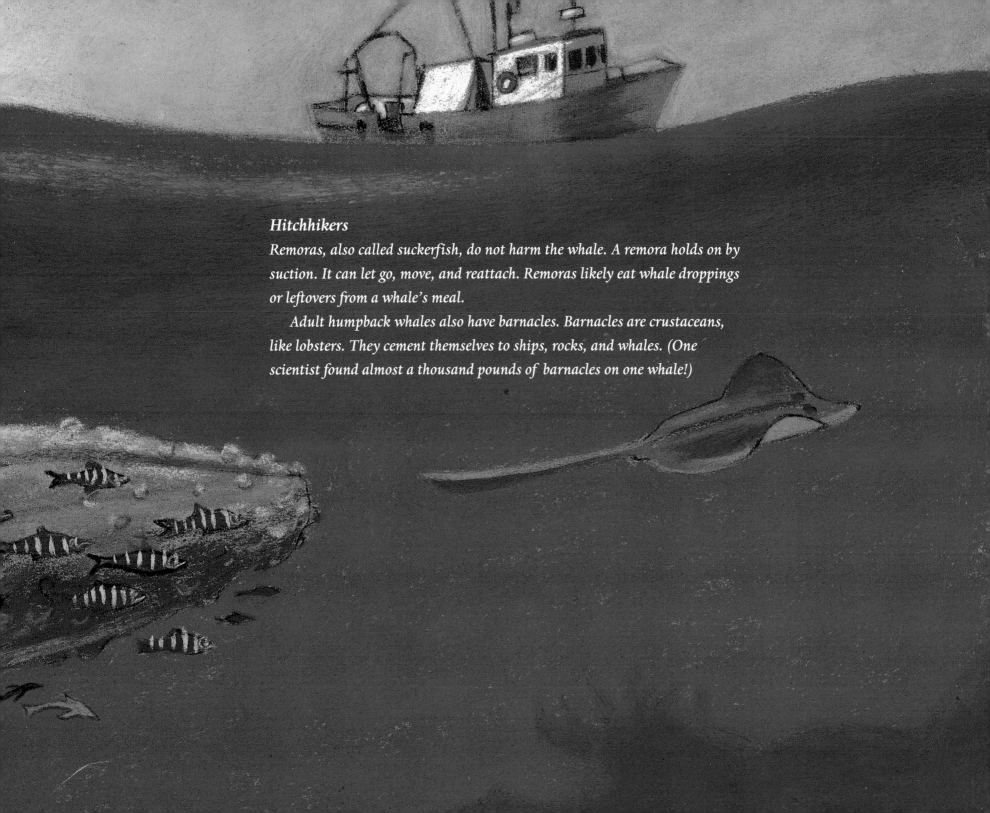

Hitchhikers

Remoras, also called suckerfish, do not harm the whale. A remora holds on by suction. It can let go, move, and reattach. Remoras likely eat whale droppings or leftovers from a whale's meal.

Adult humpback whales also have barnacles. Barnacles are crustaceans, like lobsters. They cement themselves to ships, rocks, and whales. (One scientist found almost a thousand pounds of barnacles on one whale!)

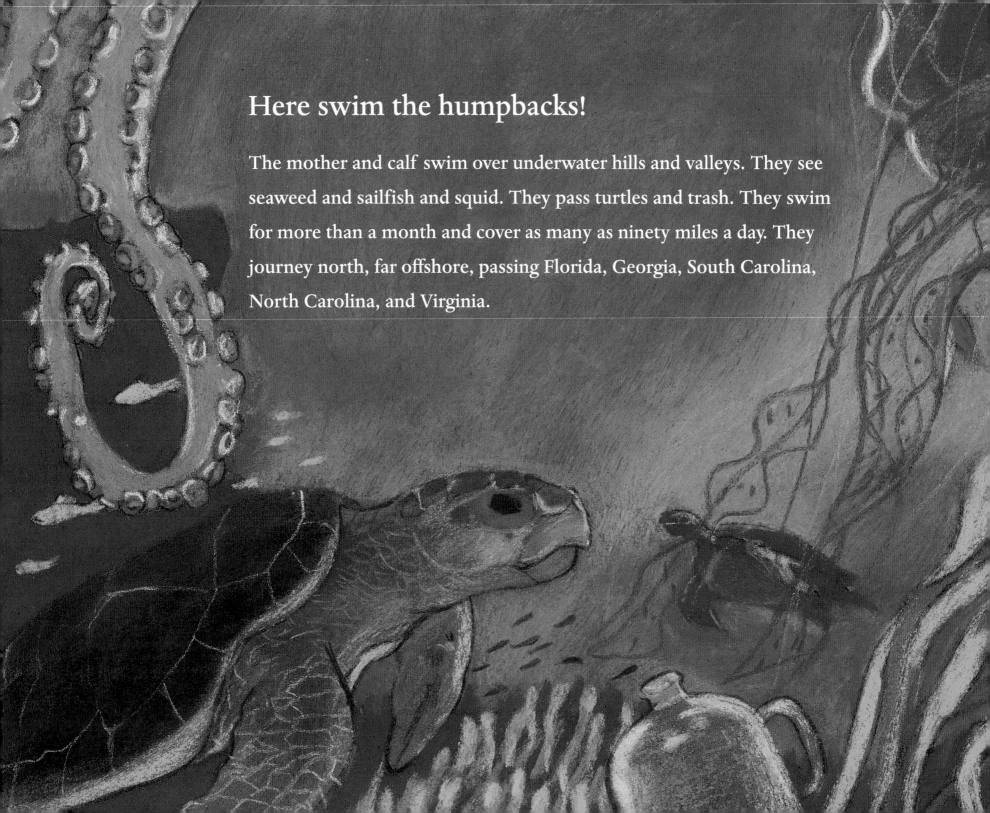

Here swim the humpbacks!

The mother and calf swim over underwater hills and valleys. They see seaweed and sailfish and squid. They pass turtles and trash. They swim for more than a month and cover as many as ninety miles a day. They journey north, far offshore, passing Florida, Georgia, South Carolina, North Carolina, and Virginia.

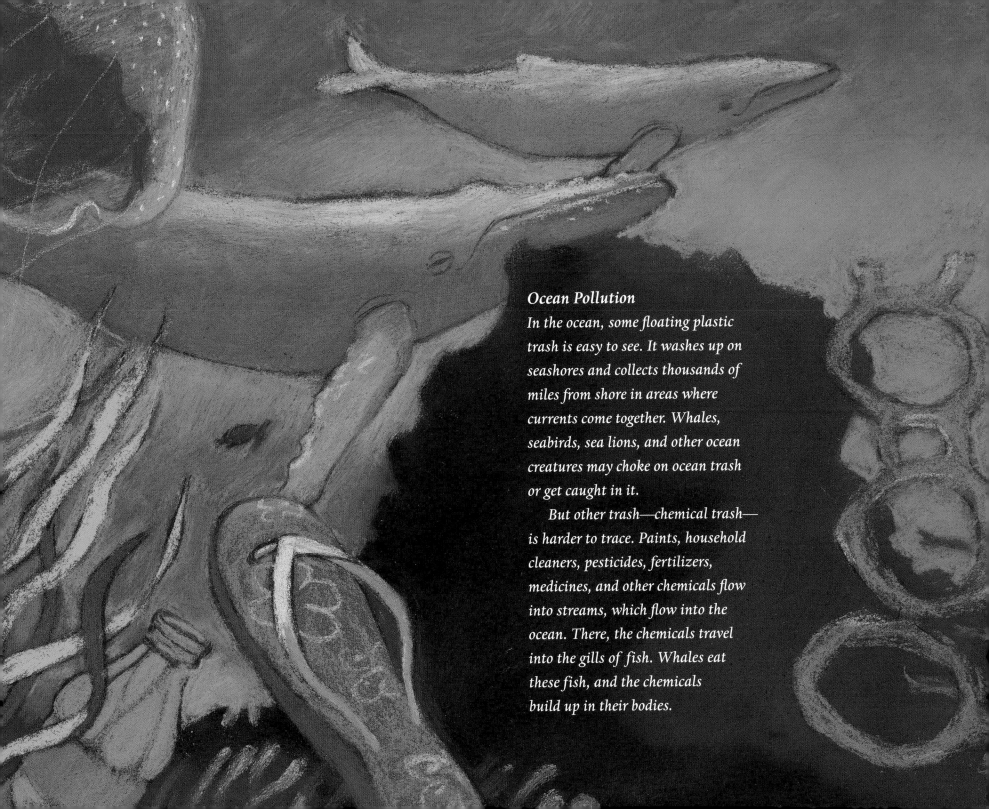

Ocean Pollution

In the ocean, some floating plastic trash is easy to see. It washes up on seashores and collects thousands of miles from shore in areas where currents come together. Whales, seabirds, sea lions, and other ocean creatures may choke on ocean trash or get caught in it.

But other trash—chemical trash—is harder to trace. Paints, household cleaners, pesticides, fertilizers, medicines, and other chemicals flow into streams, which flow into the ocean. There, the chemicals travel into the gills of fish. Whales eat these fish, and the chemicals build up in their bodies.

They swim onward, past Delaware, New Jersey, New York, Connecticut, and Rhode Island. Some waters are busy with boats. This mother and calf are lucky. They make it safely beyond the shipping lanes.

Up ahead are feeding grounds. Only a few miles—and five orcas— lie in between.

Survival Challenges and Helpers

Whales encounter many dangers as they migrate long distances. Most adult humpbacks show marks from being tangled in fishing ropes, lines, and nets. Some coastal areas have volunteer teams on call to try to remove the ropes and lines from entangled whales.

Another danger is boats, which sometimes run into whales. Moira Brown, a Canadian biologist, worked for years to convince the government of Canada to move shipping lanes—the routes the tankers take—farther away from where whales tend to swim. In 2003 Canada moved some of its Bay of Fundy shipping lanes to help protect North Atlantic right whales, one of the world's rarest whale species.

Here come the orcas!

The orcas approach. The mother humpback tries to shield her calf—
but they are five, and she is one. An orca grabs the calf's tail and jerks
the calf backward. Flapping flippers, the calf struggles. The mother
humpback slams her head into the orca's side. It opens its mouth,
and the calf shakes loose.

 The mother and calf shoot forward. They are free! The orcas fall back.
Bleeding but safe, the calf will heal—but he will have a mark from this meeting.

Flipper Hand

*Humpbacks have longer flippers than other whales. (*Megaptera, *the first part of their scientific name—*Megaptera novaeangliae*—means "big winged," a nod to humpbacks' large flippers.) Humpbacks' flippers are about a third of their body length. They are not soft like a fish's fins. Hidden in the humpback whale's flippers are bones, similar to the bones of a human hand.*

Where are the other humpbacks?

The calf is tired. His mother is weak from hunger. But up ahead, past Cape Cod, a marvelous meal awaits. Slim fish, half buried in sand, rise up and school. They are the sand lance of Stellwagen Bank.

The Ocean Stew

Not every mouthful of ocean water is full of food. The ocean has areas that are like deserts, with very little life near the surface. Other areas swarm with krill, herring, capelin, and sand lance. One of these food-filled areas, in summer, is Stellwagen Bank, an underwater plateau, or bank, off the coast of Massachusetts. Here, cool, nutrient-rich water hits the underwater plateau and then flows to the surface. This upwelling attracts plankton, plankton-eating creatures, fish such as sand lance, and finally, whales and seabirds.

Here are the other humpbacks!

Five humpbacks dive. They release lungfuls of bubbles. Up, up the bubbles rise. To avoid the bubbles, the fish bunch together. Jaws open, the humpbacks surge upward. Mouths meet fish, and pleated throats stretch wide.

Humpback Groups

A group of whales is called a pod.
Humpback whales sometimes form
pods to feed and socialize. But they
rarely form permanent groups with
the same members all the time.
Groups form and usually break
apart after a few minutes or hours.
In Alaska, however, some pods of
humpback whales hunt together
for days at a time.

After many miles and months, the mother finally feeds. She lunges, mouth open. Water drains out through her comblike baleen, leaving the fish inside.

For now the calf watches. He is still nursing. But in the next few months, he will learn to feed on fish. He will fill up on krill until his droppings are pinkish from what he's eating.

What's That Pinkish Stuff?

Whale feces (droppings) are cloudy strips over a foot long. If the whales are feeding on krill—pink, shrimplike crustaceans—their feces are pinkish. Whales eating fish have feces that are brown. Scientists following whales may use a small net to scoop up the feces. The chemistry of the feces can tell them about the health of the whales.

In late autumn the air chills. Snow falls on land, on sea, and even on the backs of whales.

Here go the humpbacks!

Migration time is here. The mother and calf leave. This journey, like the last, has dangers. Orcas hunt—but orcas are little threat to the calf now. He is almost thirty feet long and weighs over nine tons! His flippers and tail are powerful.

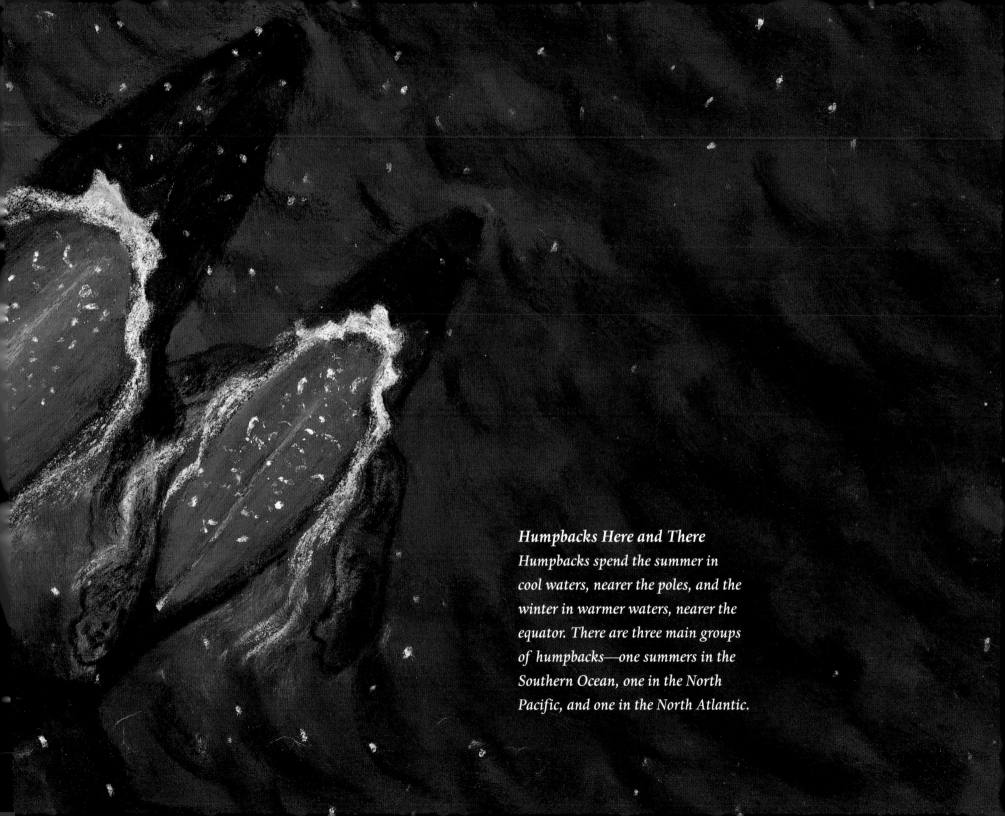

Humpbacks Here and There
Humpbacks spend the summer in cool waters, nearer the poles, and the winter in warmer waters, nearer the equator. There are three main groups of humpbacks—one summers in the Southern Ocean, one in the North Pacific, and one in the North Atlantic.

In December the mother and calf arrive
in warm Caribbean waters.

Here are the humpbacks!

Here sing the humpbacks!

Here, humpbacks are born.

Next spring, the calf will find his own path northward.
His mother will travel, too. And this year, or the next,
she will guide another calf on its very first migration.

THE GREAT MIGRATION

Humpback whales live in every ocean on Earth, and people on every continent can see their spouts. The whales in this book live in the Atlantic Ocean. They winter in the Caribbean, from the Bahamas to the Grenadines. Large numbers gather at Silver Bank and Navidad Bank, two shallow areas between the Dominican Republic and the Bahamas. Silver Bank is a protected area, a sanctuary for marine mammals.

In spring these whales migrate north. The mother and calf in this book travel to Stellwagen Bank, in the Gulf of Maine. Whale-watching boats from Boston, Gloucester, Plymouth, Bar Harbor, and other New England cities and towns visit Stellwagen Bank. How do scientists know that the same whales show up in both places? They keep catalogs of photos of whales sighted. Each whale's tail and dorsal fin have unique markings.

To travel from Silver Bank, near the Dominican Republic, to Stellwagen Bank, near Massachusetts, humpbacks travel 1,700 miles (2,700 kilometers). Other humpback populations travel even farther. Biologist Kristin Rasmussen found that humpbacks that winter near Costa Rica travel at least 5,100 miles (8,200 kilometers) to spend the summer near Antarctica. That makes the whale's journey one of the longest migrations of any mammal, on land or sea.

Studying Whales

Whales are hard to follow. The ocean is vast and whales swim long distances. For twenty-nine years Phil Clapham has studied humpbacks by traveling to where they feed and breed. But until recently he did not know much about their journey in between. In 2009 Dr. Clapham and his team attached satellite tags to several humpback whales at Silver Bank, in the Caribbean. These tags sent signals to satellites whenever the whales surfaced, and the satellites sent signals to computers. Dr. Clapham and his fellow scientists plotted the information until they could see the actual route whales took from their winter grounds to their summer grounds.

Humpbacks: Rare but Increasing

The United States government has designated the humpback whale an endangered species. Scientists estimate that there are about 50,000 humpback whales. Thanks to laws protecting whales, the number of humpbacks is slowly but steadily increasing.

For my niece Catherine: make a splash!—A. P. S.

For Daisy, who crosses water twice a day.—J. H.

Acknowledgments

Thank you to the cetacean scientists and conservationists who ride boats in rough weather, stare at computer data, and watch quiet seas, waiting for whales, hour after hour. Special thanks to Dr. Phillip Clapham, who was so generous with his knowledge—clarifying complexities, reviewing text, and sharing terrific stories. My gratitude to Katy Payne, Dr. Chris Clark, Dr. Michael Moore, and Dr. Roger Payne for answering questions for this and my previous book, *Secrets of Sound: Studying the Calls of Whales, Elephants, and Birds.* Thank you to Jeff Sayre for helpful comments on several stages of the book.

Text copyright © 2013 by April Pulley Sayre
Illustrations copyright © 2013 by Jamie Hogan
All rights reserved, including the right of reproduction in whole or in part in any form.
Charlesbridge and colophon are registered trademarks of Charlesbridge Publishing, Inc.

Published by Charlesbridge
85 Main Street
Watertown, MA 02472
(617) 926-0329
www.charlesbridge.com

Library of Congress Cataloging-in-Publication Data
Sayre, April Pulley.
    Here come the humpbacks! / April Pulley Sayre ;
illustrated by Jamie Hogan.
        p. cm.
    ISBN 978-1-58089-405-0 (reinforced for library use)
    ISBN 978-1-58089-406-7 (softcover)
1. Humpback whale—Juvenile literature. I. Hogan, Jamie, ill. II. Title.
    QL737.C424S29 2013
    599.5'25—dc23   2012000785

Printed in China
(hc) 10 9 8 7 6 5 4 3 2 1
(sc) 10 9 8 7 6 5 4 3 2 1

Illustrations done in charcoal pencil and pastel on sanded paper
Display type set in Ogre by Australian Type Foundry
Text type set in Dante Mt by Monotype
Color separations by KHL Chroma Graphics, Singapore
Printed September 2012 by 1010 Printing International Limited in Huizhou, Guangdong, China
Production supervision by Brian G. Walker
Designed by Martha MacLeod Sikkema